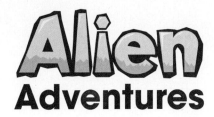

Alien Adventures

An Odd Bug

Gill Munton ● Jonatronix

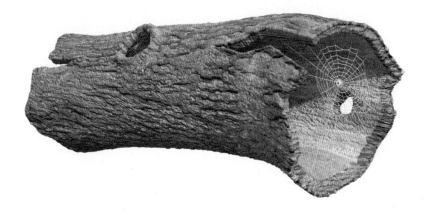

OXFORD

UNIVERSITY PRESS

In this story ...

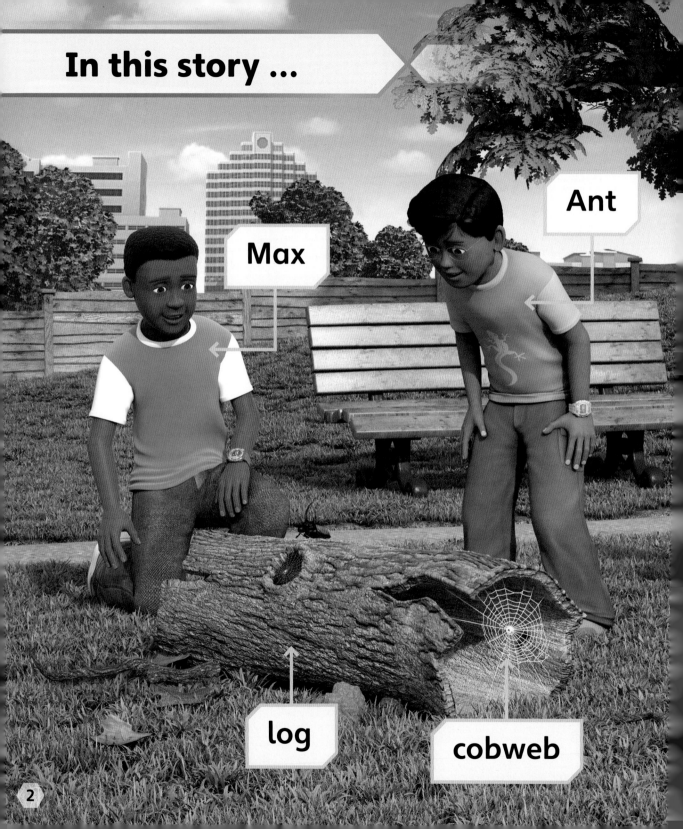

Max

Ant

log

cobweb

2

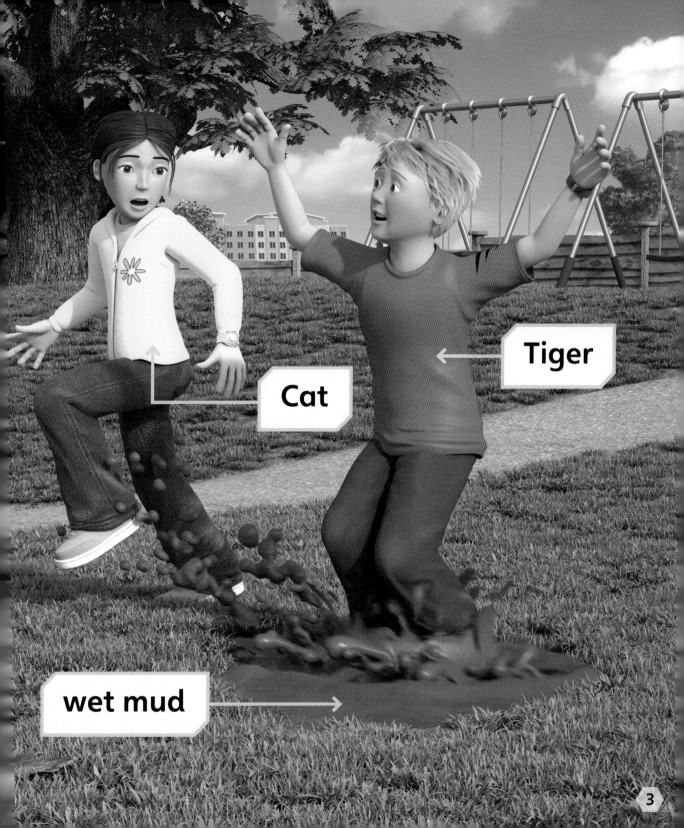

Cat

Tiger

wet mud

3

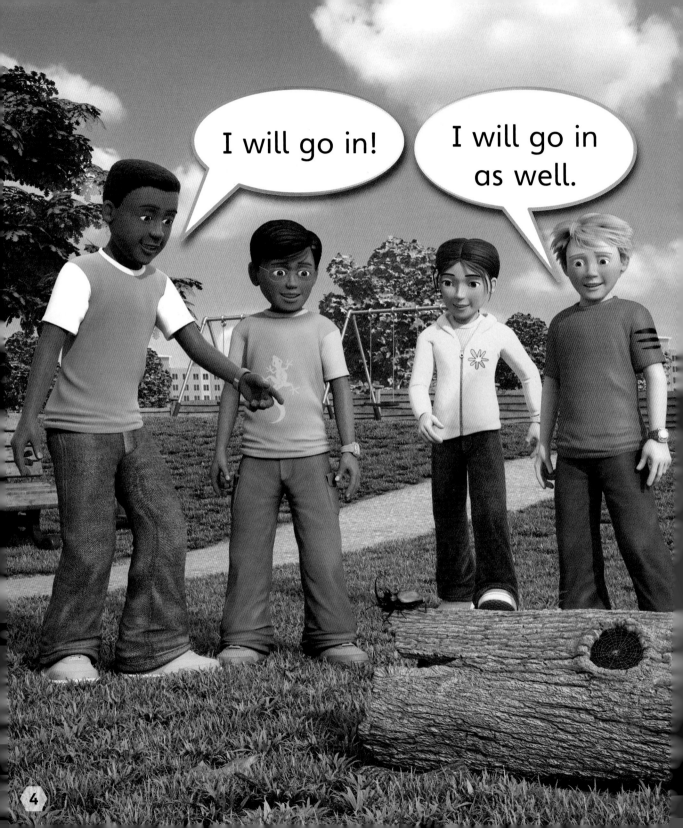

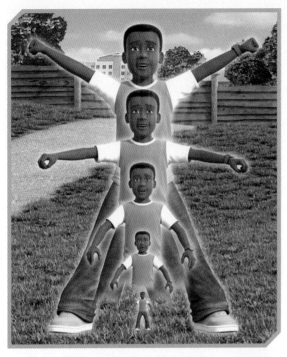

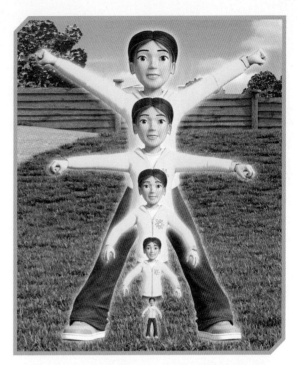

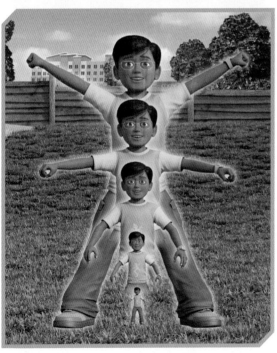

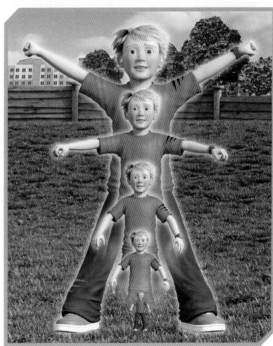

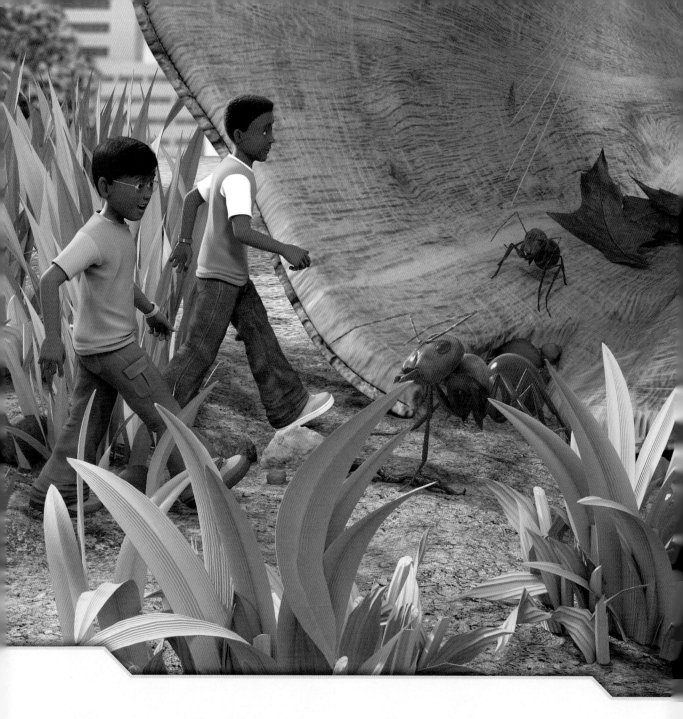

Max and Ant go in the log.

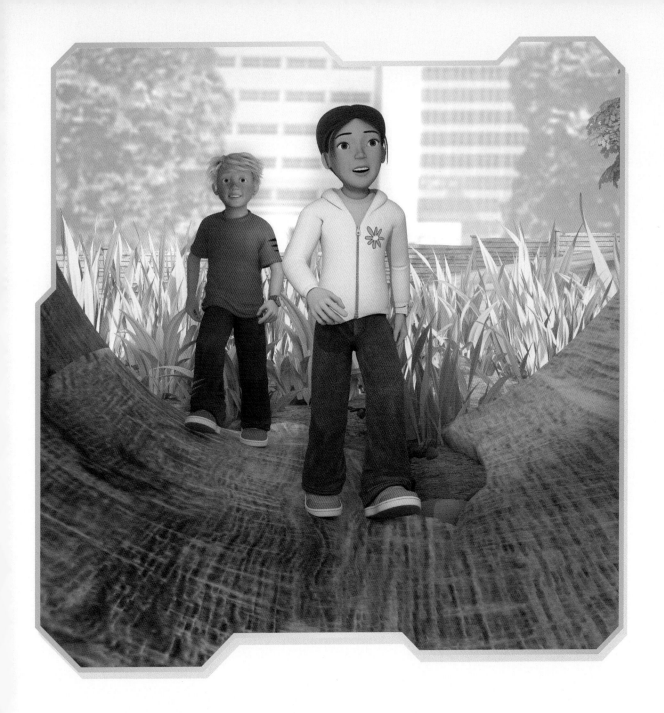

Cat and Tiger go in as well.

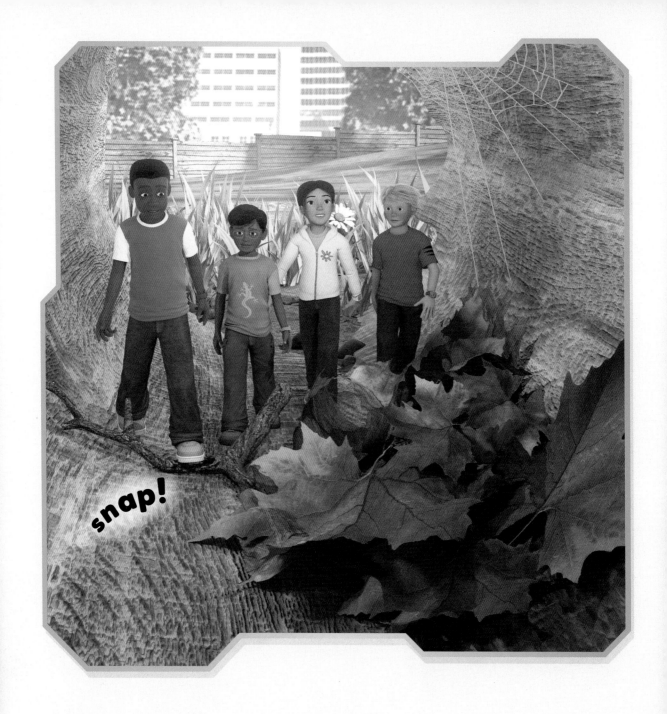

Max steps on a twig.

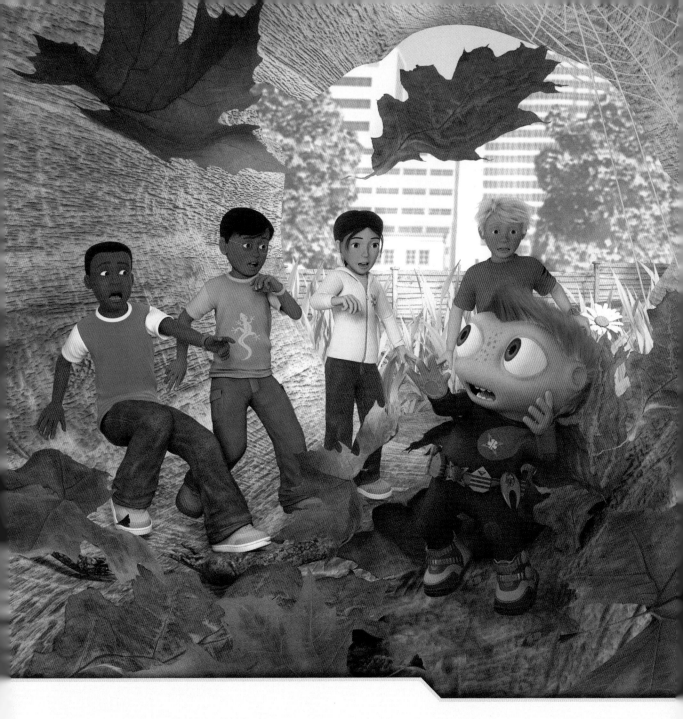

An odd bug jumps up.

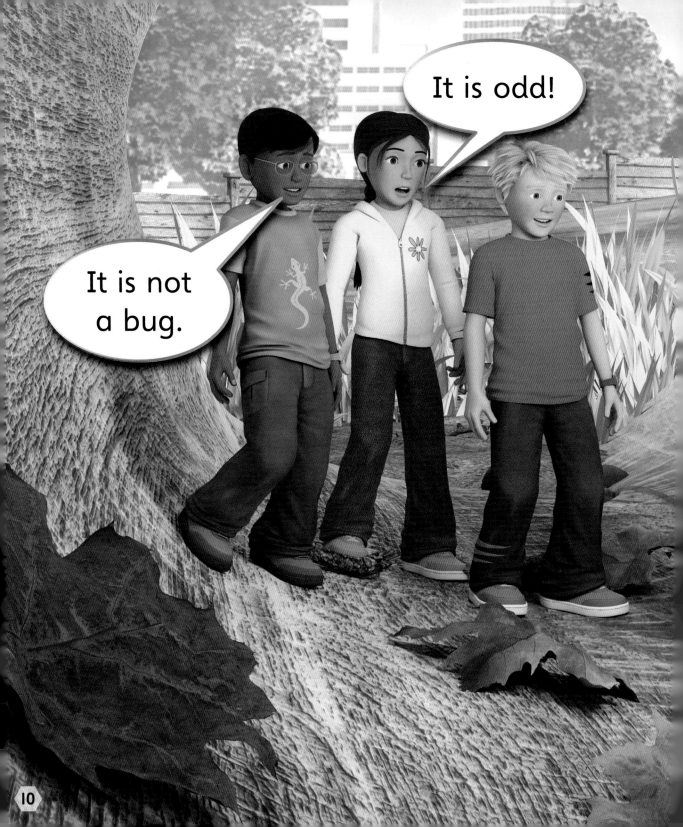

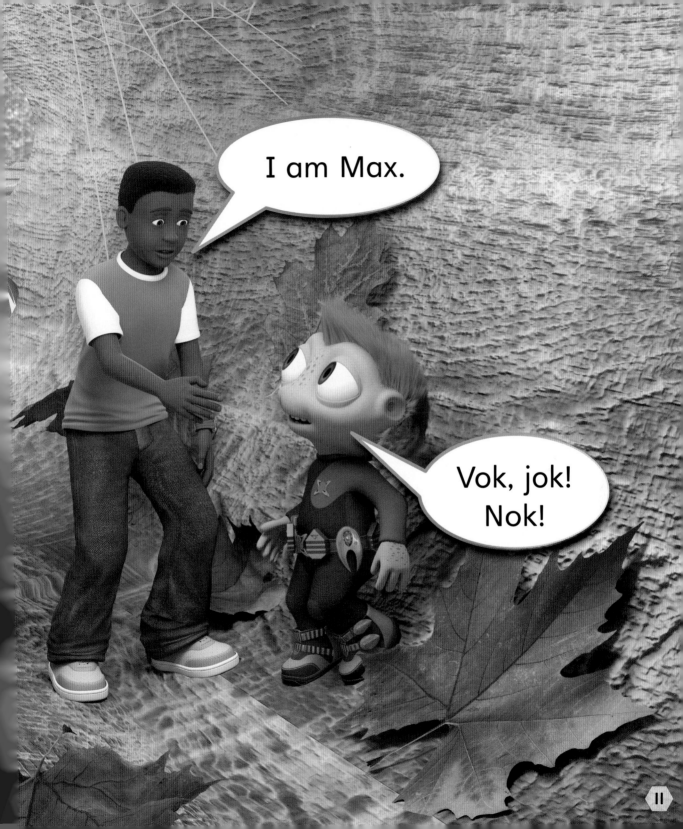

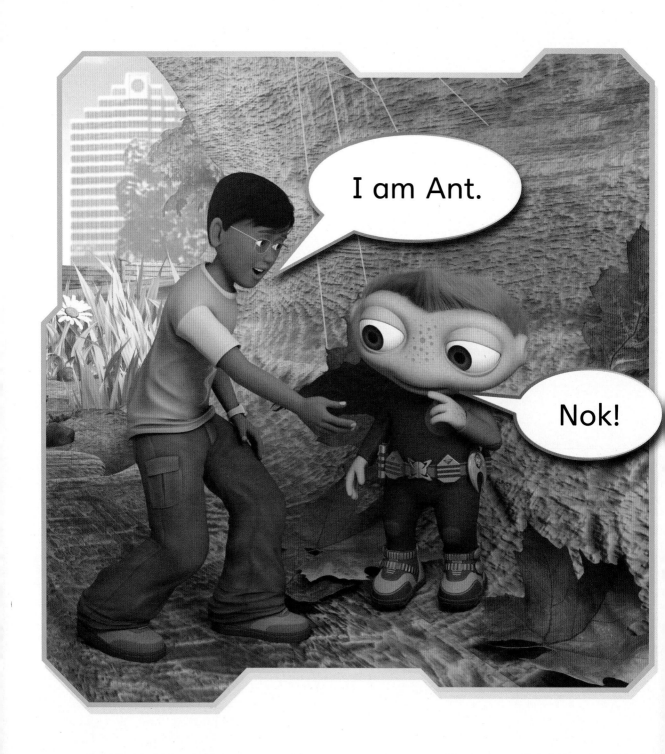

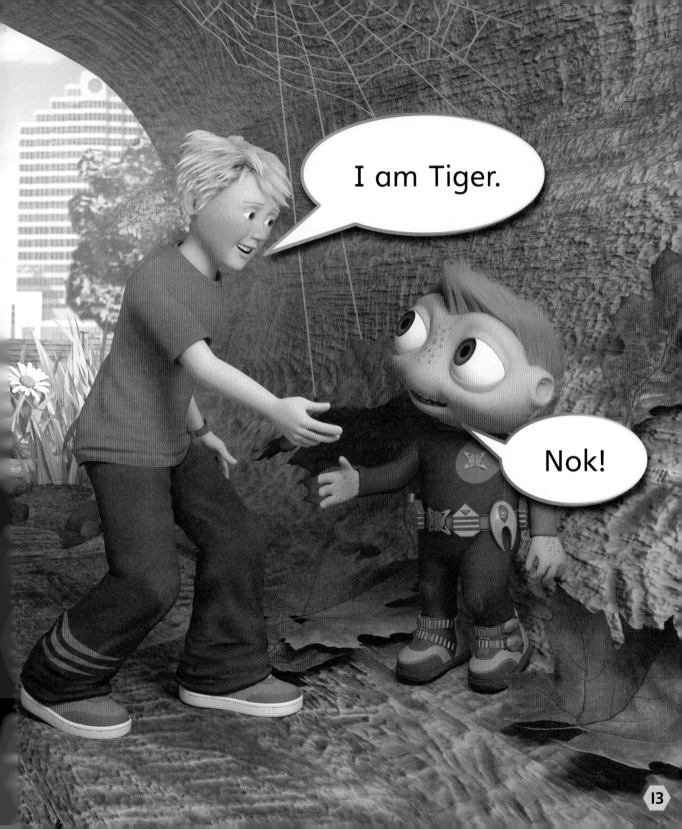

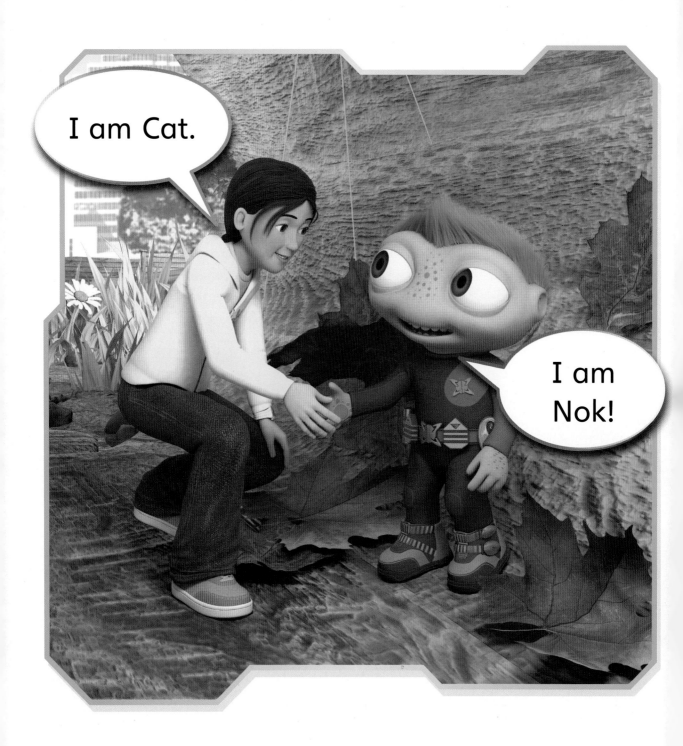

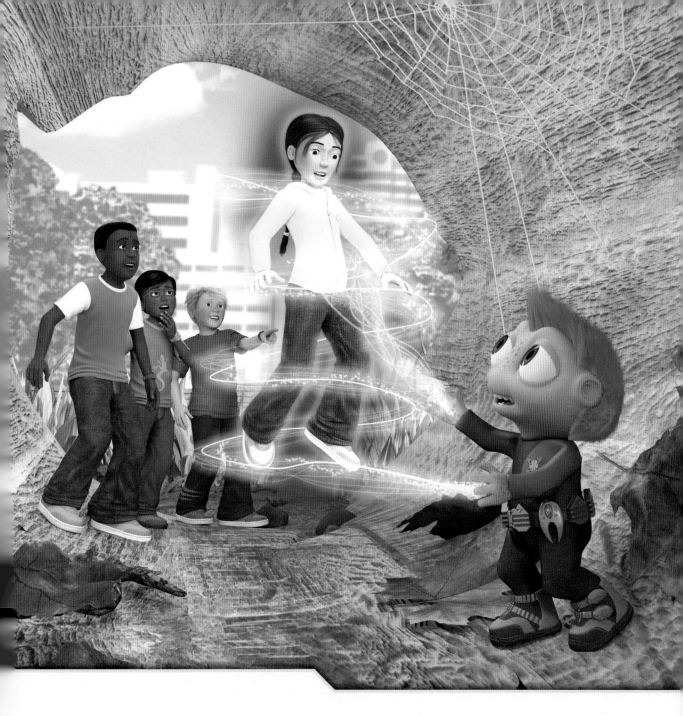

Nok is fun!

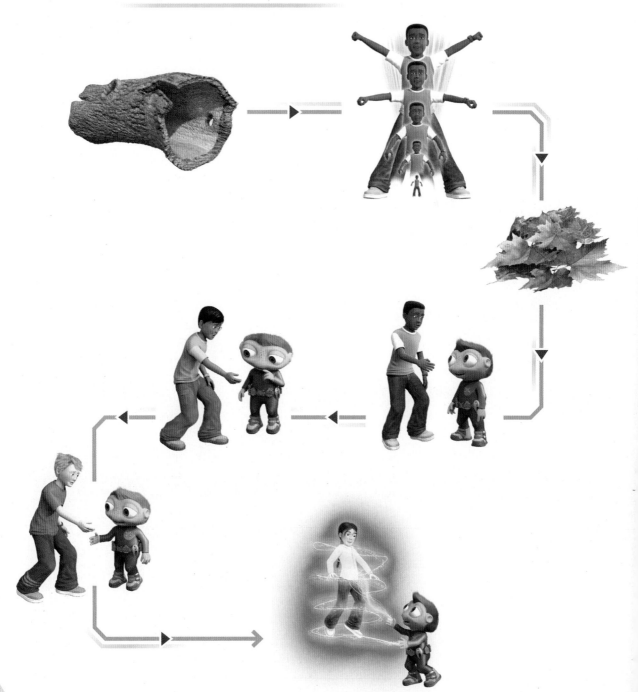